Dean Augustus Walker

The Semitic Negative

With special reference to the negative in Hebrew

Dean Augustus Walker

The Semitic Negative
With special reference to the negative in Hebrew

ISBN/EAN: 9783337419141

Printed in Europe, USA, Canada, Australia, Japan

Cover: Foto ©ninafisch / pixelio.de

More available books at **www.hansebooks.com**

THE SEMITIC NEGATIVE

WITH SPECIAL REFERENCE TO THE NEGATIVE IN HEBREW

BY

DEAN A. WALKER

WELLS COLLEGE, AURORA, N. Y.

CHICAGO

The University of Chicago Press

1896

[Reprinted from THE AMERICAN JOURNAL OF SEMITIC LANGUAGES AND LITERATURES, Vol. XII., Nos. 3 and 4. Chicago, Ill.]

TABLE OF CONTENTS.

THE SEMITIC NEGATIVE WITH SPECIAL REFERENCE TO THE NEGATIVE IN HEBREW.

By Professor DEAN A. WALKER, A.M., B.D., PH.D.,

Wells College, Aurora, N. Y.

LITERATURE.

The text used in the enumeration and citation of negative forms and constructions in the Hebrew and Aramaic of the Old Testament is that of *Myer Levi Letteris*, John Wiley and Sons, New York, 1892. On doubtful points comparison has been made, where possible, with the Baer and Delitzsch text, but it seemed best to base the work on a text already completed for the entire Old Testament. The quotations in Arabic are from the *Corani Textus Arabicus*, editit Gustavus Fluegel, Lipsiae, 1881. In addition the following books have been consulted constantly:

Gesenius, *Hebrew and English Lexicon of the Old Testament*, new edition, by Francis Brown, with the coöperation of S. R. Driver and C. A. Briggs. Boston, 1891, *sqq.*

Gesenius, *Hebrew and English Lexicon of the Old Testament*, edited by Edward Robinson. 3d ed. Boston, 1849.

Gesenius, *Handwörterbuch*. 8th ed. Leipzig, 1878.

Gesenius-Mitchell, *Hebrew Grammar*, 1893.

Gesenius-Kautzsch, *Hebräische Grammatik*. 22d ed. Leipzig, 1878.

Gesenius-Rödiger, *Hebrew Grammar*. 14th ed. Trans. by Conant. New York, 1846.

Ewald, *Hebrew Grammar*. London, 1836.

Ewald, *Lehrbuch der hebräischen Sprache*. 6th ed. 1855.

Böttcher, *Ausführliches Lehrbuch der hebräischen Sprache*. Leipzig, 1866.

Green, *Hebrew Grammar*.

Stade, *Hebräische Grammatik*. Leipzig, 1879.

Kalisch, *Hebrew Grammar*.

Schroeder, *Linguae Hebraeae*.

Schroeder, *Die Phönizische Sprache*. Halle, 1869.

Stade, Erneute Prüfung des zwischen dem Phönizischen und Hebräischen bestehenden Verwandtschaftsgrades, *Morgenländische Forschungen*. Leipzig, 1875.

5

Nöldeke, *Mandäische Grammatik.* Halle, 1875.

Wortabet, *Arabic-English Dictionary.* Cairo, 1888.

Wright, *Arabic Grammar.* London, 1859.

Wright, *Comparative Grammar of the Semitic Languages.* Cambridge (Eng.), 1890.

Ewald, *Grammatica Critica Linguae Arabicae.* Leipzig, 1831.

Lansing, *An Arabic Manual.* 2d ed. New York, 1891.

Socin, *Arabic Grammar.* Leipzig, 1885.

Zimmern, *Babylonische Busspsalmen.* Leipzig, 1885.

Palmer, *The Qur'ân. Sacred Books of the East.* Vols. VI. and IX. Oxford, 1880.

Sale, *The Koran.* London, 1850.

Torrey, *Commercial-Theological Terms in the Qur'ân.* Leyden, 1892.

Delitzsch, *Assyrisches Wörterbuch.* Leipzig, 1887.

Delitzsch, *Assyrian Grammar.* New York, 1889.

Dillmann, *Grammatik der Äthiopischen Sprache.* Leipzig, 1857.

Nöldeke, *Syriac Grammar.*

Wilson, *Syriac Grammar.*

McCurdy, *Aryo-Semitic Speech,* 1881.

Delitzsch, *Studien über Indogermanisch-Semitische Wurzelverwandtschaft.* Leipzig, 1873.

Lindsay, *The Latin Language.* Oxford, 1894.

Whitney, *Sanskrit Grammar.* 2d ed. Leipzig, 1889.

Lanman, *Sanskrit Reader.* Boston, 1884.

F. Max Müller, *Lectures on the Science of Language.* 2d series London, 1864.

Strong, Logeman and Wheeler, *The History of Language.* London, 1891.

Halévy, *Mélanges d'épigraphie.* Paris, 1874.

INTRODUCTION.

The purpose of this article is

a. To present in comparative tables all the forms of negative particles or words used as such in the Semitic languages.

b. To classify these forms according to origin in (1) form, (2) fundamental idea, (3) syntactical usage.

c. To show the relation of different particles to each other in the same language and in different languages.

d. To trace the development and composition of certain negatives from more primitive forms and ideas.

e. To discuss some previous views as to origin and composition and offer some new explanations of forms.

I.

OF THE NEGATIVE IN GENERAL.

Forms for the expression of the negative idea are found in every language. There is probably no negative idea that could not be expressed by some affirmative but circumlocutory formula; but the negative particle serves the purpose both of convenience and force, and in some forms is as old as language itself. It is, in fact, a necessity, and as language grows, the primitive negative differentiates or new forms are found to express new and different shades or degrees of force in the negative idea. Tracing this development historically we find its first expression in gesture, in which form it is found even before language begins, as may be noted in the development of the individual human being, is seen in the animal, and may be inferred for the human race if the theory of evolution be accepted. The kicking and balking of a horse, the growl of the dog when you approach to take from him his mutton-bone are emphatic expressions of dissent. The first is gesture pure and simple, like the shrug of the shoulder or the shake of the head in man. The growl of the dog might be called a vocal gesture, and is a second stage in the development of negative expression, a step toward a vocabulary which man in articulate language has carried to completion.*

In the mere animal, the negative is an expression of emotional dissent, in man it may be emotional or intellectual. As emotional, both gesture and voice by modifications and combinations, the shrug of the shoulders, the toss or shake of the head, the facial expression, the inflexion of the voice, may add to the idea of dissent the element of scorn, contempt, disgust or indignation. As intellectual, the idea of negation by use of a differentiated vocabulary may be modified to express relations of time as continuous, previous or subsequent (as in *never, not yet, no longer,* which are expressed in some languages by single primitive words), or of subordination, condition, contingency, etc. In man, therefore, we have the three steps in the expression of dissent or negation, the gesture, the natural impulse of the vocal

---

* On the chronological order of development of the affirmative and negative sentence, see *The History of Language,* by H. A. Strong, W. S. Logeman and B. I. Wheeler, p. 102.

organs, and the intellectual choice of words in a more or less
extended vocabulary. In this vocabulary of the negative, we are
inclined to believe that in every language, at least in every group
of related languages, there will be found at least one negative
particle originating in this primitive natural impulse of the vocal
organs expressing itself in what we have called the vocal gesture
of dissent. The remaining particles have originated in ideas
more or less closely associated with that of negation, or even from
ideas originally quite unrelated. In accordance with this view
we may classify the vocabulary of the negative under four heads:

$a.$ Negative of pure dissent.

$b.$ "   by association of ideas.

$c.$ "   " transference of idea.

$d.$ "   " suggestion or attenuation.

The fuller explanation of these terms will appear in the
classification of the Semitic negatives, but it is in order here to
discuss the meaning and appropriateness of the first designation,
the "negative of pure dissent."

The negative of pure dissent is the particle resulting from the
vocal gesture of dissent. It might be expected that this particle,
originating in the primitive natural impulse of the vocal organs,
would be the same for all men, and be found common to all
languages, but such is not the fact. We do find, however, in a
particular group of languages a common negative stem, which by
its appearance in all the members of the group, is shown to be
the primitive negative for that family. Such a negative is found
for the Indo-European family in the negative stem n, and in the
Semitic family in the stem l, which appears in every member of
the group. There may or may not be a connection between the
two families and a significance in the fact that the negative in
each is a liquid,* but the question why the Indo-European chose
n and the Semitic chose l belongs back of philology to the realm
of psychology, along with the question why among some peoples
the common gesture of dissent is a sidewise shake of the head,
while among others it is the backward toss. The Englishman
and the Arab are agreed in expressing assent by a forward

* For the exchange of *yodh* for *lam* in Western Aramaic and Syriac, and for *nun* and
lam in the Babylonian Talmud and Mandaic as proformatives of the imperfect, see
Wright's *Comparative Grammar of the Semitic Languages*, p. 183.

inclination of the head, and are agreed, too, that dissent is the opposite of assent, but the Englishman, regarding the gesture of assent as an up-and-down motion, finds the opposite in a right-and-left motion; while the Arab, regarding the affirmative as a forward and downward nod, finds its opposite in a backward and upward toss of the head. Can psychology explain this? Is it perhaps that in the Englishman's dissent there is more of deliberation, more of the intellectual, while in the Arab's dissent the emotional prevails, and the backward toss of the head expresses primarily that the offer or the proposition offends his pride or is beneath his notice? For the Arab, too, has a sidewise shake of the head, which is also intellectual, but with him expresses, not dissent, but doubt: "I do not understand the question, please repeat." This distinction, however, does not follow strictly the ethnic or linguistic lines of separation. The Greeks, perhaps through contact with Orientals, have adopted their gesture of dissent, as indicated in the words κατανύω and ἀνανύω, while the Armenians, belonging to the same family, though oriental in all their surroundings, have yet preserved the sidewise shake of the head. I am told by an Armenian friend, however, that among the Armenians also, the toss of the head as a negative gesture is assumed as a matter of fashion or coquetry for a short period by young brides and by girls of a marriageable age.

II.

In the following table a view is presented of the Semitic negatives arranged according to roots and in doubtful cases according to probable etymological relationship. The table does not claim to be complete, for some of the other languages if read with as broad an interpretation of the term *negative* might yield as large a list as the Hebrew; while in the Hebrew list are some whose claim to be called negatives might be disputed, such as the אֵם and מָה, though their cognates in the Arabic cannot be disputed as negatives. Especially doubtful as to etymological relationship are the é and a-a of the Assyrian and an, ak, anbi and anbe of the Ethiopic, while the proper position, in the table, of Assyrian ul and Ethiopic albo is not certain

Table A.—Comparative Table of Semitic Negatives.

HEBREW	ARABIC	ASSYRIAN	SYRIAC	BIBL. ARAM.	ETHIOPIC	PHOENICIAN
לֹא , לוֹא	لَا لَمْ لَمَّا لَنْ	la, la-a (=la)	لَا , خُد	לָא		
בְּלֹא	بِلَا , كَلَّا إِلَّا , أَلَّا				አል0 (?)	
	لَيْسَ	laššu (?) ul	خَمه	לֵית אַל אַי Talmudic	እ—	אל אי
אַל (אֶל) לְוִל+(י or א) אִי אַיִן ,אֵין ,אִין בַּל		a-a(?), θ(?)			አነ, አኅ አነለ, አነ-ዐ	Punic in Plautus en, yn
	بَل بَلَى	balu(m) ba-la				בַּל ,אִיבַל
בְּלִי בִּלְתִּי בִּלְעֲדֵי טֶרֶם אֶפֶס זוּלָתִי פֶּן פִּי מָה אִם	مَا إِنْ لَكِنْ , لَكِنَّ غَيْرٌ نَوْ		قَحْخُ	אִם, אָן לָהֵן		
לוּ, לוּא מֵן (?)			خَمَ			

Classifying the negatives according to the root ideas, we have the following table, illustrated most fully in the Hebrew. Where it is desired to represent a root that appears in different forms in several languages, we use English letters, and so also in treating of vowel sounds common to several forms:

Table B.—Psychological Distribution of Negatives.

a) Negative of pure dissent:
   1. Indo-European — *n*.
   2. Semitic — *l*.

b) Negative by association:
   1. Diminution or decay, בַּל from stem בלה *to waste away*.
   2. Cutting off, טֶרֶם.
   3. Cessation, אֶפֶס.
   4. Removal, זוּלָת from root זִל *to remove*.
   5. Change, פֶּן from stem פָּנָה *to turn away*, غَيْر *other*.
   6. Separation, בַּד (?)

c) Negative by transference of force:
   1. Conditional, Heb. אִם *if*, Arab. إِنْ *if*.
   2. Interrogative, Arab. مَا, Heb. אַיִן.

d) Negative by suggestion:
   1. Emptiness, רִיק.
   2. Vanity, הֶבֶל.
   3. Falsehood, שָׁוְא.
   4. Waste or desolation, תֹּהוּ.
      Cf. the implications in such English expressions as *almost, hardly*, etc.

III.

THE NEGATIVE OF PURE DISSENT.

Of the Semitic negatives, by far the most frequent and the one which alone is found in every language of the group is the simple particle of dissent or pure negation, of which the essential part is the consonantal sound *l*. That this is the essential element in all the score or more of forms in which it appears is shown in the great variety of vowels by which its pronunciation

is assisted and by the fact that its vowel may be long or short
and may follow or precede. Thus the vowel

is long in לֹא, לוּלֵי, לָ, לֵיֹסֶ, כֵלָّ, إلّ, أَلّ, Assyr. la-a,
ﻻ, كُﺪ, كُﻤﺪ, لَﺍ, لِيﺡ;

is short in אַל (אֶל), לֵם, לַّﺎ, לֶן, אֵל(?) (Phœn.), Assyr. ul,
and ኣልቦ;

is a in לָ, לֵיֹסֶ, כֵلّ, إلّ, أَلّ, ﻻ, كُﺪ, كُﻤﺪ, لَﺍ, אֵל, לֵם,
لَّﺎ, لَن, אֵל(?) (Phœn.), ኣልቦ;

is e in לוּלֵי, לِيﺡ; ĕ in אֶל, u in ul, and o in לֹא.

It follows the consonant in most forms, but precedes in אַל,
Assyrian ul, and ኣልቦ (albo).

The simplest form in which this negative appears is the
Arabic ﻻ, which, though there is in it an *aliph* of prolongation,
employs this only as a support for the *fatḥa*, for it is to be noted
that in the colloquial, to which rather than to poetry we must go
for analogies of primitive values, the word is as often pronounced
short; and so always in بَلﻻ, where the accent, so far as it has
any, falls on the first syllable. Without this supporting *aliph*,
which is not a *hamza* though often sounded as such, the negative
would consist of a single consonant with its vowel point standing
alone, a combination that nowhere occurs in Arabic, a particle
consisting of a single consonant and its vowel always attaching
itself as proclitic or enclitic. The negative as proclitic is found
in the Ethiopic አ and Hebrew אִ and in Indo-European in-,
un-, alpha privative, etc., but in Arabic would be liable to confusion with the prepositions or the ﻝ of the jussive or the asseverative ﻝ. A single consonant must attach itself to a following
word or take a vowel letter, as in ﻲ and ﻣﺎ, and ذُو, ذِى, ذَا.
In Assyrian the syllable is in some cases definitely indicated as
long by the repetition of the vowel (la-a), but elsewhere is
undetermined. The Hebrew, Syriac and Biblical Aramaic always
point it long in the forms in which the vowel follows the consonant, but it is to be remembered that this can at most indicate the
usage in pronunciation at the time when the vowel points were
invented, and while the Hebrew has adopted a sufficient variety

of vowel points to indicate fine shades of distinction in its vowel sounds, the Syriac shows that the same pointing may in different branches of the language be given very diverse pronunciation, while the three vowel points of the Arabic, a comparatively late addition to the alphabetic writing, are quite inadequate to distinguish the variety of vowel sounds found in the spoken Arabic of today, and probably when invented, only roughly represented the three principal groups of vowel sounds then employed. The utter confusion of values in the English vowel system is an extreme illustration of what is true in a measure in Arabic, and though the Hebrew system of vowel points is more minute, it is an artificial system and can at best represent the pronunciation of Hebrew as it was at a comparatively late date, and possibly also over a limited area.* It can furnish no indication of primitive Semitic pronunciation nor decide, as against the phenomena of modern colloquial Arabic, that the particle *l* always employed a long vowel. The sound which we give to the Hebrew ḥôlēm is as difficult for the modern Syrian Arab as French *u* is for an Englishman. It may have been equally so for the ancient Israelite, and the length of the vowel sound in the negative particle may have been determined as in the modern colloquial Arabic by the amount of emphasis thrown upon the word or the character of the emotion expressed.

The significance of the longer writing of the Assyrian particle, la-a, is not clear, nor that of the longer form of the Hebrew לוֹא. Does the longer form indicate anything as to length or emphasis in the original pronunciation, or is it in the Assyrian merely a scribal device for making the line come out right, or is it accidental in both, or is it a personal scribal characteristic? The following table and discussion on the Hebrew particle will present some of the facts, though they may discover no important principles. The most obvious fact is that the long form is found most frequently in composition with the interrogative particle הֲ . For comparison therefore the table gives the number of cases where the short form is found with הֲ and where the long form is found without הֲ including a few cases where it is found with the preposition בְּ .

---

* *Cf.* the local variations in pronunciation of the German affirmative particle *ja.*

In the accompanying table it is seen that the long form occurs with הֲ interrogative 141 times, but the same הֲ takes the short form nearly as many times, namely 128, while the long form occurs without הֲ 35 times. From this it is evident that the particle הֲ does not determine the form of the negative. Is the long form then characteristic of certain (*a*) books, (*b*) authors, (*c*) periods of time or (*d*) qualities of style and subject matter, as poetical or prose, historical or liturgical?

As to (*a*) books, it is seen that in the compound, 12 books use only the long form, while 5 use only the short, or, leaving out those books in which the occurrence is so rare as hardly to be considered characteristic, and taking the two books of Samuel as one and the two books of Chronicles as one, we find that Judges, Job, and Chronicles use the short form exclusively, occurring respectively 13, 14, and 19 times, while Samuel is characterized by the exclusive use of the long form, occurring 34 times. But in 15 books both forms occur, some showing a preference for the one, some for the other. The distinction therefore can hardly be one of books.

Is the distinction (*b*) one of authorship? Ezekiel, which is confessedly the work of one author, uses the two forms in the compound impartially, 8 to 8. So also do Amos and Ruth, each 2 to 2. Jeremiah indeed shows a decided though not exclusive preference for the long form, 14 to 3, and in the uncompounded particle, uses the long form 19 times as against 5 times in the two Isaiahs, which

Table C.—*Occurrences of* הֲלֹא , הֲלוֹא *and* לֹא.

	חלא	הלוא	לוא
Gen. ...	5	8	1
Ex......	3	1	...
Lev.....	...	...	1
Num....	6	2	...
Deut....	3	1	...
Josh....	1	2	...
Judg....	13	...	...
1 Sam...	...	20	2
2 Sam...	...	14	...
1 Kgs...	9	6	3
2 Kgs...	17	12	...
Isa......	7	18	5
Jer......	3	14	19
Ezek....	8	8	2
Hos.....	...	...	...
Joel	...	1	...
Amos...	2	2	...
Obad....	...	4	...
Jon.....	...	1	...
Mic.....	...	5	...
Nah.....	...	...	...
Hab.....	...	4	...
Zeph....	...	...	...
Hag.....	...	1	...
Zech....	1	5	...
Mal.....	...	3	...
Ps......	11	1	...
Prov....	3	1	...
Job.....	14	...	...
Cant....	...	...	...
Ruth ...	2	2	...
Lam....	...	...	1
Eccles...	1	...	1
Esther..	...	1	...
Dan.....	...	...	...
Ezra....	...	1	...
Neh.....	...	3	...
1 Chron.	4	...	...
2 Chron.	15	...	...
Total...	128	141	35

make the next most frequent use of it. Testing the question on the commonly accepted documentary division of Isaiah we have the following table of occurrences, showing that both forms occur in each main section and often in close proximity: Long, 8:19; 28:25; 37:26; 40:21'; 42:24; 43:19; 44:20; 45:21; 48:6; 51:9, 10; 57:4; 58:6, 7. Short, 10:8, 9, 11; 29:17; 36:12; 44:8; 57:11. The distinction therefore cannot be one of authorship.

As to (c) period, we find that the widely separated books of Judges and Chronicles agree in the exclusive use of the short form, while Daniel (?), Ezra and Nehemiah, approximately contemporary with Chronicles, use only the long form.

As to (d) literary style and subject matter, we find that the prophets from Hosea to Malachi, with the exception of Amos and Ezekiel, who are impartial, and Hosea, Nahum and Zephaniah, who furnish no data, prefer the long to the short form, 56 to 11, while the wisdom literature of Psalms, Proverbs, Job and Ecclesiastes prefers the short form by 29 to 2. But on the other hand, Judges and Job, as diverse as possible, in these respects agree in the exclusive use of the short form, while Judges and Samuel, similar in subject matter, are at opposites, Samuel using only the long form. Equally fruitless is the effort to find any euphonic or syntactical distinction, as appears, e. g., in Isa. 65:1,

$$\text{מְדְרָשֻׁתִי לְלוֹא שָׁאָלוּ}$$
$$\text{נִמְצֵאתִי לְלֹא בִקְשֻׁנִי}$$

where in the same verse, by the same author, in the same construction and practically the same euphonic conditions, we have the two forms. We are left to the conclusion therefore that in some books the long form is due to arbitrary scribal preference, and in others to scribal inconsistency and carelessness perpetuated by scribal scrupulosity, or else, wherever it occurs it was intended originally to indicate some emphasis whose force is now lost to us, the further definition of which in a dead language and in the absence of any direct ancient testimony, would be mere conjecture. The view that the long form is a less corrupted relic of an original triliteral verb form * fails to account for its preser-

* Presented by Dietrich in *Gesenius' Wörterbuch*, see לֹא, criticised by Böttcher, *Lehrbuch der hebräischen Sprache*, § 532, p. 340, footnote 1.

vation in the same author and in close proximity with the shorter form, and there is no good ground for supposing that this negative particle ever was a noun.* To the question whether the noun or the verb was the earliest of the parts of speech the true answer is "neither; but the interjection," and in the negative particle *l* we have preserved one of the original interjections.

In the use of this common particle *l*, three members of the Semitic family, the Hebrew, Biblical Aramaic, and Phœnician have differentiated a form to distinguish between prohibition and deprecation, using for the latter the form אַל in which the vowel precedes the consonant. No such distinction is found in Arabic, Assyrian, Syriac, or Ethiopic. The explanation of the form lies, perhaps, in this, that a form beginning with a short vowel is less explosive than one beginning with a consonant and can less easily be prolonged for emphasis than one ending in a vowel. Hence its effect is milder and it serves to express the milder feeling of entreaty. In actual usage, however, the two forms are sometimes found in the same sentence with consecutive verbs or nouns where no distinction of force can be assumed, *cf.* Lev. 10:6. Where, as in this case, the לֹא follows the אַל, it might be considered a case of לֹא used to perpetuate another negative, a construction common enough with ي in Arabic, but extremely rare with לֹא in Hebrew. But in Prov. 27:2, where the negatives are used with nouns, we have the reversed order, from which we must conclude that in some cases, at least, no distinction is made. We have also two cases, Prov. 12:28 (with noun) and Cant. 7:3 (with verb) where, if the rendering of the Revised Version be accepted, אַל is not jussive but declarative.

It is with some hesitation that the Assyrian u l is classed with the *l* negatives. The word is usually considered as the construct state of a noun, u l l u, "non-existence, nothingness," from a verb, a l â l u, "be feeble, nought," *cf.* Zimmern, *Busspsalmen*, p. 83, and others.† But if אַל has any connection with לֹא, it seems equally probable that ul is another form of la from which it differs in usage even less than אַל from לֹא.‡ The particular force of ul has

---

* See to the contrary Gesenius-Kautzsch *Hebräische Grammatik*, § 100, 1.

† Delitzsch, *Assyrisches Wörterbuch*; Idem, *Prolegomena*, 133, Halévy, *Mélanges d'épigraphie*, 165.

‡ *Cf.*, however, Assyrian a l in proper name Al-duglâ-niśô, II Rawl. 63c., 42.

not been determined. Delitzsch is inclined to make the distinction that ul is used only in principal clauses while la is found in both principal and subordinate constructions and with all the parts of speech susceptible of negation.* The suggestion is due to Dr. Geo. R. Berry, of The University of Chicago, that there may be in ul an emphasis of contrast, the suggestion being based on several passages,—Tig.Pil. I., cols. 1:72; 5:38; 7:68, 70: Ašurnaṣ. 1:43, 108,—where the king in his treatment of a conquered city or the rebuilding of a temple does *not* follow the precedents: "that city (contrary to the usual custom) I did *not* destroy, devastate and burn with fire."

In Syriac, alongside of ܠ we find ܠܐ, a stronger negative compounded of ܠ and ܗ.

In Arab. ليس Syr. ܠܝܬ, Bib. Aram. לית and Assyr. laššu, we have compounds of this primitive *l* and the noun of existence *yeš*. The Aramaic of Daniel and Ezra fails to compound the two parts but has לא־אית and the Hebrew has לא יֵשׁ and אֵין יֵשׁ. The Arabic, on the contrary, not only compounds the parts, but losing sight of the original character of the parts, treats the compound as a verb, defective indeed but capable of considerable inflection for person and number.

IV.

NEGATIVE BY TRANSFERENCE.

Under this term is included the use of the interrogative and conditional particles as negatives, represented by the Arabic ما and أنْ and the Hebrew אַיִן and אָם.

The transition of a particle from an interrogative to a negative force is a process depending upon the frequency of a certain use of the interrogative known as the rhetorical question. The rhetorical question is one of the most emphatic means for conveying a positive idea, and even before the introductory particle has lost its interrogative character, the force of the sentence as a whole has become that of a negative assertion. Thus in English, "What have I done?" spoken in a tone of indignant surprise means emphatically, "I have done nothing (for which I should be

* Delitzsch, *Assyrian Grammar*, 1889, § 143, p. 352.

blamed)." So in Hebrew, "Is thy servant a dog, that he should do this thing?" is an emphatic disclaimer of a disparaging impu- tation. In modern Arabic, a man excusing himself from some mishap, exclaims, šu beddi 'amil, "What did I (or, "do I") want to do?" = "What could I do (under the circumstances)?" the equivalent of the English plea, "I couldn't help it." In all these cases, it is the rhetorical question, expecting no answer because assuming that there can be but one answer, and hence very emphatic. The question for information may be very urgent, but can never be emphatic because by its very nature it implies doubt, an inquiring rather than an assertive state of mind. But the rhetorical question is used only where the speaker knows that there can be but one answer, and that one in accordance with his own view. Hence it is in force equivalent to a statement of axiomatic value, that is, a very positive and emphatic one. Hence the particle converted from this rhetorical interrogative use to do duty as a negative will be somewhat more emphatic than the ordinary negative. This will be shown in a discussion of the Arabic ما.

There is, however, another process by which the negative may be derived from the interrogative value. The interrogative may be, not substantive, but adverbial, i. e., it may ask, not "what?" but "where?" or "how?" and this may pass into a negative force by the following process. So long as the query "where?" is in the mind, there is a consciousness of the absence or *notness* of the object sought, and the longer the query remains unanswered, the stronger becomes the sense of *notness*, and this sense of *notness*, at first local, if the search be continued long enough, will become a sense of absolute non-existence. Hence the sense of *whereness* and *notness*, inseparably associated, come in time to be identified, and the same particle may then serve as the sign of either. This has, in fact, occurred in the Semitic languages, and is possibly represented in the Hebrew particle אִין and its cognates.

The negatives derived from the interrogatives are all based upon the interrogative roots, *m* and *ay*. The former as a negative is confined to the Arabic, with possibly a few cases in Hebrew (*cf.* under מַיִן in Table E, Syntactical Constructions); the latter is most frequent in Hebrew and Ethiopic, and appears possibly in the Assyrian, but is not found in Arabic. We will first develop the negative of the *m* root.

A. *The Arabic Negative* مَا.—Like the negative consonant *l* of pure dissent in the Indo-European, the interrogative root *m* is found with different vowels under different circumstances. For the impersonal or neuter it appears in Arabic as مَا and for the personal as مَنْ, but this in the colloquial modern Arabic has also the pronunciation مِين with the *kesra* lengthened perhaps to distinguish it from the preposition مِنْ. In Hebrew we find it with the *a* vowel for the impersonal, מָה and the *i* vowel for the personal מִי. In this long *i*, the Hebrew corresponds to the colloquial Arabic, which raises the question whether both may not be a degeneration from the original *a* which the written Arabic has preserved in both personal and impersonal مَنْ and مَا.

Of these two forms, it is only the impersonal that has passed into the interrogative force. The reason for this is plain. There is indeed no logical reason why the rhetorical question, " *Whom* have I on earth beside Thee?" should not come to be read as a negative statement, "I have no one on earth beside Thee," as well as that the question, " *What* could I do?" should come to mean, "I could do nothing." But it must be remembered that the transition of the particle from the interrogative to the negative force depends entirely upon the frequency of its use, that is, the rhetorical question must be used so frequently as to become a stereotyped formula for a negative thought. The personal interrogative in rhetorical question has never attained to such frequent use as to become a stereotyped formula, and it is for the same reason that in Hebrew even the impersonal מַה cannot be regarded as a negative except in the two places in Cant. 8:4, where the structure of the sentence for the sake of analogy with 2:7 and 3:5 demands it.

In treating this particle مَا we note first that as distinguished from the adverbial and qualitative interrogative أَيْ, this is the substantive interrogative, and as such may be nominative or accusative, and as nominative may be either subject or predicate nominative, and as accusative may be the direct object or the second accusative appositive to the object, or the adverbial accusative.

The following cases from the Quran taken first as interrogative will illustrate these uses. Sur. 86:10 فَمَا لَـهُ مِ.ن قُـوة (وَلا ناصِر). Neglecting the second part, we may read, "For what (is there) to him of power?" in which the لَ is subject nominative, a rhetorical question which easily becomes the negative statement, "For he has no power," which is continued and determined as negative by the negative وَلا ناصِر "nor helper." Compare with this the similar construction in Hebrew, 1 Kgs. 12:16, מַה־לָּנוּ חֵלֶק בְּדָוִד וְלֹא־נַחֲלָה בְּבֶן־יִשַׁי where, however, we are to regard the first clause as remaining a rhetorical interrogative,* because the form is not so frequent in Hebrew as in Arabic, and the לֹא in Hebrew, unlike the لا in Arabic, is not used to continue another negative. Sur. 97:2, وَمَا ادرَاك مَا لَيلَة القَدر "And what can show thee what the night of power is?" Here the first مَا is plainly subject nominative to ادرَاك and has not departed from its interrogative force, since to do so would leave the verb without a subject; while the second مَا is as clearly a predicate nominative to the nominal sentence of which لَيلَة القَدر is the logical subject, and could not be rendered as a negative without breaking the connection of the clauses.

For مَا as predicate nominative compare also Sur. 70:41 وَمَا نَحن بِمَسبو قِين "And what are we among (or us) those prevented?" cf. German: Was für .... sind wir? Here the نَحن is the logical subject and مَا the predicate nominative, but the sentence becomes "We are *not* among those prevented."

Of the three accusative uses, that of the direct object is rare. In Sur. 53:3, وَمَا يَنطِق عَن الهَوى "And what does he speak out of lust?" = "He never speaks out of lust," the مَا is (originally) direct object of يَنطِق.

In the two clauses immediately preceding this, مَا ضَل صَاحبكم وَمَا غَوى, "Your companion does not err nor does he go astray," the two مَا's traced back in the same way to the rhetorical inter-

---

* Cf. also 2 Sam. 20:1, where אֵין is to be similarly explained.

rogative give us adverbial accusatives, "*In what respect* does your companion err and *in what respect* does he go astray?" Here the original interrogative force of لَ is attested by its use in the second clause, since had the first لَ been merely a negative, it would more probably have been continued by ﻻ. A good case of accusative of measure or cognate accusative is found in Sur. 74:49, فَمَا يَنْفَعُهُمْ شَفَاعَةُ الشَّافِعِينَ "For what will the intercession of the intercessors avail them?" = the intercession of the intercessors will avail them nothing, will *not* avail them.

In this way most of the negative uses of لَ may be traced back to the interrogative, but there remain a few in which the particle in the construction in which it stands cannot be rendered as interrogative because the sentence without it is fully supplied with all it can contain of subject and predicate nominative, and object and adverbial accusative. Thus in Sur. 74:34, وَمَا يَعْلَمُ جُنُودَ رَبِّكَ إِلَّا هُوَ "And not does anyone know the armies of thy Lord except He," the لَ cannot be subject nominative because a personal subject is required; it cannot be predicate nominative because the verb is transitive; it cannot be object accusative because that is supplied by جُنُود ; and there is no occasion for an adverbial accusative. The sentence therefore could not be originally a rhetorical question, and the لَ could be nothing else than a negative. Here then is a clear case of لَ as having become a negative before entering into the sentence. It has come to be a negative particle in and of itself, and capable of being used like ﻻ in sentences that cannot be read as rhetorical interrogatives. Such extreme cases, however, are rare, and nearly all sentences with لَ show a trace of their interrogative origin.

What now is the peculiar force of the negative لَ as distinguished from ﻻ. It has been customary to say, following the native grammarians, that لَ is used with the perfect, generally of past time, and is more emphatic than ﻻ. Thus Lansing* has "لَ = not, negative of the absolute present and of the perfect." It has also been said that the restrictives† إِلَّا, etc., following a negative prefer the negative لَ. But while this is true in

* Lansing, *An Arabic Manual*, § 72, p. 123.
† Ewald, *Grammatica Critica Linguae Arabicae*, Part II., pp. 201-3.

many cases, it is too general and the exceptions are too numerous.
ما is used freely with both the perfect and imperfect tenses and
in speaking of past, present and future time. And as for إلا, it
is found more often, indeed, preceded by ما, but so frequently
by أن and sometimes by لا, that we can hardly suppose that it
is the إلا that calls for a ما, but something further back than
the mere presence of a restrictive. We must find some more fundamental distinction between ما and لا. The following examples will show how varied is the use of ما as to form of verb used
and time referred to, and will serve as a means by which to arrive
at the basal principle.

    1. With perfect tense of past time, Sur. 67:10, ما كنا في
اصحاب السعير "We would not have been among the fellows of
the blaze." Sur. 53:11, ما كذب الفواد ما رأى "The heart did
not belie what it saw," referring to a definite past event. Sur.
53:17, ما زاغ البصر وما طغى "The sight did not turn aside nor
waver," referring to an incident of Muḥammad's vision.

    2. With perfect tense of present time (?) Sur. 26:208, وما
اهلكنا من قرية الا لها منذرون "And we never destroy (Palmer),
destroyed (Sale), a town except it has (had) warners." For a
clearer case, in which Palmer and Sale are agreed in rendering
the verbs in the present, and the parallelism supports this rendering, we have Sur. 53:2, ما ضل صاحبكم وما غوى "Your companion does not err, nor does he go astray." In v. 3 the thought
is carried out with ما and the imperfect, وما ينطق عن الهوى
"nor does he speak out of lust." The words occurring at the
opening of the surah are an assertion of the prophet's veracity
and credibility with reference, not to some past occasion, but to
what he is about to say; hence we may fairly assume that present
time is intended and that the three verbs, two in the perfect and
one in the imperfect, are used without distinction.

    3. With imperfect referring to present time Sur. 67:19, ما
يمسكهن الا لرحمن "Not does there hold them (the birds) up,
except the Merciful."

    4. With imperfect referring to the future, Sur. 92:11, وما
يغنى عنه ماله اذا ت دى "And not shall his wealth avail him

when he falls down" (into hell), referring to the day of judgment, hence, evidently future, *cf.* also Sur. 74:49 above.

In nominal sentences, also, the ما is used with equal freedom
as to time, though for the past for definiteness we usually find
the verb كان expressed, as in Sur. 67:10, ما كنا فى اصحاب
السعير where we might have had ما نحن but for the ambiguity
as to time.

In the present we have, Sur. 81:25, وما هو بقول سيطان رجيم
"And it is not the word of a pelted devil." In the future, Sur.
82:16, وما هم عنها بغائبين "And they will not be among the
absent from it," *i. e.*, from the broiling in hell on the judgment
day.

From the above and similar passages we find that ما is used
with the perfect tense for present and past time, with the imperfect for present and future time and in nominal sentences for
present and future time. The distinction between ما and ى therefore has primarily nothing to do with the tense used or the time
referred to, but must be sought in the nature, *i. e.*, in the original
force, of the particle itself. We shall find that all the phenomena of ما, the tenses used, its preference for present and past
time, its greater emphasis as compared with ى, are sufficiently
explained by its origin as an interrogative and its transition to
the negative force through the rhetorical question.

The rhetorical interrogative as a substitute for a positive assertion of a fact is a stronger method of conveying the thought, but
can be safely resorted to only where the facts are so well known or
at least are so far matter of general consent that the speaker can
be reasonably sure that the answer, should one be returned,
would accord with the impression he intends to convey. If he is
addressing his own partisans, he may venture the rhetorical question with more freedom than in speaking to opponents. Such a
question answered in the affirmative when a negative answer is
called for would be fatal to the purpose of the speaker.

On what classes of facts now, may a speaker venture to put
his teachings in the interrogative form? There are two such
classes, (*a*) facts of the past and present of which his hearers
may reasonably be supposed to have positive historical knowledge

or present experience, including such facts in revealed religion as have had their event in the past, which, though not matter of human experience, have yet been accepted with equal positiveness as facts, cf. Sur. 74:30, and (b) general truths holding good for all time and doctrines as to the future on which there is a general consensus in the moral and religious consciousness of the hearers.

Of course in either of these cases the speaker in his confidence in his own position may be led to substitute his own assurance for that of his hearers, as when in Sur. 53:17 the prophet relates with great positiveness the details of his vision, forgetting that these could not be matters of experience with his followers nor of general acceptance as history, but relying on the unquestioning faith of his followers in himself as sufficient to inspire them with as much assurance as personal experience could have furnished.

As illustrative of confidence in historical facts the prophet in Sur. 39:51, referring to the destruction of Thamud and Ad, exclaims, فما اغنى عنهم ما كانوا يكسبون "What then did that avail them which they had been engaged in acquiring?" It was an unquestioned tradition that the tribe of Thamud had amassed great wealth. It was equally certain that a terrible destruction had befallen them. Hence the conclusion followed that their wealth was of no avail, and to the prophet's question, "Did that wealth save them?" there could be but one answer, "Most assuredly not."

So also in regard to the fate of the unbelievers at the judgment day, Muhammad, using the imperfect tense in this case, could ask with assurance, "What will the intercession of the intercessors avail them?" and again, "What will his wealth profit him when he falls down (into hell)?" To these also there could be but one answer, "Nothing"; for free grace at the judgment day is something unknown to Islâm, and no doctrine is more emphasized in the Quran than that the awards of the future life will be apportioned strictly in accordance with what men have deserved by their conduct in this life, so that neither intercession nor wealth will have influence on the decision. (Cf. Dr Chas. C. Torrey's Commercial-Theological Terms in the Qur'ân.)

We can now see why, as the grammars have noticed, لا is found more frequently with past and absolute present time, and is more emphatic than ي. It is more emphatic because the rhetorical question in which it originated is a more emphatic way of conveying a negative idea than the simple negative sentence; and it is found more frequently with the past and absolute present, not because the particle as such prefers one tense or time rather than another, but because matters of history and present personal experience can be more safely appealed to than matters still in the future, and offer a wider range of facts. The future is, of necessity, less certain than the present and past, and it is only where faith gives to the future something of the reality of experience, that لا can properly be used of future time.

It cannot be maintained, however, that this distinction is always in the author's mind where لا is found. Even in the Quran there are found such sentences as Sur. 39:67, وما قدروا

الله حق قدره "But they have not rated God at his true power," where it is difficult to cast the thought in an interrogative form, or to see any special force in the negative. In later writings and in colloquial Arabic we must expect to find لا and ي used with still less discrimination; yet even here, trained and careful writers and speakers, though ignorant of the basis of distinction, will feel a difference and instinctively choose the proper particle according to this law which the grammarians have roughly formulated.

In this discussion of the Arabic لا, we have illustrated the principal steps by which an interrogative particle undergoes transition to a negative force. The transition of لا from the interrogative to the negative is very simple and direct, involving only two steps, (a) the transition of force and (b) the forgetting of the original force so far as to allow the use of the particle as a negative in constructions where the interrogative could not stand. Here with لا the process stops, and as a negative it never becomes anything more than the particle *not*. We will now follow out a similar process in the Hebrew, in which there are more steps, and where the interrogative particle not only becomes a negative particle, but even a noun of *nothingness*.

B. *The Hebrew Negative* אֵין.—Of the three interrogative
stems, *m*, *ay*, and *ha* or *a*, while the Arabic has developed a negative from the substantive interrogative *m*, the Hebrew has
chosen for the same process the qualitative interrogative *ay*, from
which it has developed a negative which occurs quite as frequently in Hebrew as the لَ in Arabic. This negative is אַיִן,
construct state אֵין. To obtain this form, the Hebrew has added
an element *n* to the stem *ay*, and welded the two together so
thoroughly as to lose sight of the original parts and to treat the
compound as a simple stem, as the Assyrian and Syriac seem to
have treated in the same manner some ת formations of verbs, and
as the Arabic has undoubtedly dealt with the *l* and *yes* in its
inflection of لَيْس. The derivation of the Hebrew אֵין from the
stem *ay* is not, therefore, so simple as that of the negative لَ
from the stem *m*.

Two principal explanations have been given of the negative
אֵין. The first is that of the school of Gesenius, which seeks to
find for every form a nominal or verbal root, as in its attempt to
make the particle לֹא a relic of some noun* or triliteral verb,† and
the Assyrian u l, a contraction of the verb a l â l u, to be feeble,
nought, and also finds wherever it can a relation between Semitic
and Aryan roots. In accordance with the first purpose, it bases
אֵין upon a hypothetical root אֵוֶן, and by reversing the radicals
connects it with the extant verb נוּא, *to say* "*no,*" and perhaps
with נוּע, *to nod*, which is found possible on the analogy of the
Indo-European *ne* and *in-* or *no* and *un-*. In pursuance of
the second tendency' it makes this נוּא and אָנֵי to be related to
the Indo-European negative stem *n*.‡ It then drops the ן from
אֵין to get the form אֵ on the analogy of the *a* privative from *αν*
in Greek, and even goes so far as to derive the interrogatives
אַיֵּה and أَي from the negative by dropping the ן.

The second explanation has been presented clearly by Bött-
cher‖ who rightly finds the basis of אֵין in the interrogative stem
ay but with some hesitation accounts for the ן as a nunnation.

* Mitchell's *Gesenius' Hebrew Grammar*, 1893, p. 255, and Gesenius-Kautzsch, *Hebräische
Grammatik*, 1878, § 100, 1.
† Dietrich in Gesenius' *Wörterbuch*, criticised by Böttcher, *Lehrbuch der hebräischen
Sprache*, § 532, p. 340, footnote 1.
‡ Böttcher's *Lehrbuch der hebräischen Sprache*, § 532.
‖ *Ibid.*

This derivation from the interrogative is adopted in Driver and Brown's new edition of *Gesenius' Lexicon** where, however, no explanation is attempted for the וֹ.

Before offering a third explanation, it is in order to point out the objections to these two views. The old view of Gesenius is open to suspicion as a forced attempt to explain the form in accordance with an assumption that all forms of speech necessarily have their origin in either nominal or verbal roots, an assumption sufficiently answered in our discussion of the origin of לֹא. The attempt to see in the three letters of אַיִן the radicals of a triliteral root can at best carry the derivation back no further than the triliteral stage of the language, which is a late stage arrived at only by a process such as is still going on in English in the adoption of regular preterites for irregular verbs and regular plurals for irregular nouns. Again, to identify the וֹ with the *n* of the Indo-European negative, and after thus making it a radical and the strongest one in the triliteral root, to allow the dropping of it on the analogy of the dropping of the *v* from ἀν- in a privative of the Greek is quite unwarranted; first, because the *n* of the Indo-European has its counterpart in *l*, not in אַיִן; secondly, because the *v* of αν in Greek and Sanskrit was originally not a true consonant but merely a nasal vowel like final *n* in French, the nasal quality of which was more or less pronounced according as it was followed by a vocal or consonantal sound, and the dropping of which was done in accordance with well defined euphonic laws; while the presence or absence of the *n* in אַיִן and its cognates אַי of the Hebrew, אַי of the Phoenician, *yn* and *en* in the Punic of Plautus, and the ኢ (?) and the ኣይ (?) of the Ethiopic, is not conditioned by euphonic laws. The same is equally true when the negative has passed, as Gesenius would have us believe, into the interrogative.† The impossibility, on psychological grounds, of the transition in this direction, from the negative to the interrogative, will be shown later, and it being possible, the *n* of the interrogative (*cf.* Heb, בְּאֵיִן, Isa. 39:3 and Arab. اين) must be otherwise accounted for.

Böttcher's explanation of וֹ as a nunnation‡ is unsatisfactory

because it fails to explain how an interrogative could receive the
nunnation, while the admission that the element *ay* is the interrogative connects it at once with the Arabic اى and hence with
اين in which the ن followed by a vowel certainly cannot be the
nunnation.

What then is the *n* in אִין ? Accepting as the basis of the
form the interrogative element *ay*, for reasons that will be given
later, the most reasonable view as to the *n* is that it is neither
the *n* of negation * nor the *n* of indefiniteness but the demonstrative *n* which by a common psychological process appears both
in Indo-European and Semitic; in the former in Sanskrit *nu*,†
Gr. νῦν, Latin *nunc* and English *now;* and in the latter, in Heb.
הִנֵּה and the precative particle נָא, and in the Arabic اين, and هنا
and possibly in the energetic form of the verb. This particle *nu*
in Sanskrit is appended with an intensive or precative force to
the interrogative,‡ as in *ko-nu, who now? who pray?* It has
the same force in נָא appended to the verb in the Hebrew precative sentence and in doubtful and courteous question.

The interrogative in Hebrew can easily take on this precative particle, yet it can as easily omit it without affecting the
form of the question. Whether it should be used or not would
depend therefore originally upon the earnestness of the speaker,
but later might become so stereotyped as to lose its special force.
This would depend upon the habit of mind of the people as a
whole, so that it might prevail more among the Hebrews than
the Phœnicians, just as the rhetorical question with *m* prevailed
more among the Arabs than among the Hebrews, so that with the
former it became stereotyped as a negative while with the latter
it failed to do so.

Beginning then as אִירַּנָא = אִירֵּנָא and اين, we have the
vowel of the *n* preserved in both. But as the Hebrew lost its
case endings, so this vowel also, being unprotected, was lost, the
more so because the *n* could, though with difficulty, fall back
upon the preceding diphthong, giving the form אַין. A similar
loss of the final vowel in colloquial Arabic reduces the أَيْن to

---

* For the contrary view see Ewald, *Hebrew Grammar*, tr. London, 1836, p. 288.

† Whitney, *Sanskrit Grammar*, §504, and Lanman, *Sanskrit Reader*, pp. 138 and 200.
Cf. also, Lindsay, *The Latin Language*, p. 615.

‡ Lanman, *Sanskrit Reader*, p. 138; Whitney, *Sanskrit Grammar*, § 504.

أَيْنَ, pronounced *āyn*, but unspellable in Arabic because the vowel system has not been sufficiently developed to indicate the sound of Hebrew *çērē* to which this exactly corresponds. This is often further corrupted in the modern colloquial, perhaps by metathesis of *yodh*, to *wāyn* and this sometimes still further to *fāyn* (*cf.* the opposite movement of ϝ in Greek as it weakens from the sound of *f* or *v* to *w* and finally disappears). But since the form אַיְן, in which the *yodh* still has something of consonantal force, is not agreeable to the Hebrew ear, the *yodh* must find a helping vowel after the manner of the so-called segholates, or change the vowel before it for one with which it can coalesce into a pure vowel sound. This leads to one of three forms. Either (*a*) the *yodh* takes as a helping vowel its cognate vowel *ḥīrēq*, giving the form אַיִן or (*b*) there is a modification of the preceding *pāthāḥ* to *çērē* with which the *yodh* more easily coalesces, giving the form אֵין, which being shorter serves for the construct state and exactly corresponds in sound to the unspellable colloquial Arabic *āyn*, or (*c*) the preceding *pāthāḥ* is heightened to *qāmēç*, and the *yodh*, changed to *waw*, takes for its helping vowel *seghol*, giving the form אָוֶן.

We have then from this interrogative stem *ay* and the precative or demonstrative *na* the forms أَيْنَ (colloquial اِين , وِين , فِين) אִידְּנָא, אֵין, אַיִן and אָיֶן, of which the last three have passed into the negative force. To these, as negatives of cognate origin, we may add the Phœnician *yn* and *en* (Punic dialect in Plautus)* and probably the Ethiopic አĬ, አን (for አĬን) አĬ.ና and አĬ-ናፈ; and from the same stem *ay* without the *na* we have the Heb. אַי (rare), Talmudic אָי, Phœnician אי (no pointed Phœnician texts have been found by which to determine the voweling) and the first part of the compound אִיבַל, Ethiopic ኡ and possibly the Assyrian a-a and ዐ.

Having traced the development of the form of אֵין, it needs but a few words to trace the transition of the idea from the interrogative to the negative force. The process is the same as in the case of مَا, but while in مَا the transition is made through the rhetorical question using the substantive interrogative *what?*

* Schroeder, *Die Phönizische Sprache*, 1869, p. 211, § 116, *b*.

in אָין, it is developed from the qualitative or adverbial *where?*
and not only through the rhetorical question, but possibly also
through the question for information. The former, however, is
certainly the more common and gives the more direct transition.
The rhetorical question, Isa. 33:18*b*, אַיֵּה סֹפֵר אַיֵּה שֹׁקֵל אַיֵּה סֹפֵר
אֶת־הַמִּגְדָּלִים "Where is he that took account, where is he that
weighed (the tribute), where is he that counted the towers?"
conveys in strongest terms the exultant thought of the speaker
that the Assyrian who had come up against the city is gone, is
destroyed, in short, *non est.*

In a less direct way, the אַיֵּה־נָא that asks for information
may become אָין, *whereness,* which implies the absence or the
nothingness or the emptiness and gives us by successive steps the
אַיִן of nothingness and the אָוֶן of vanity, worthlessness and sin.
This transition of an adverbial interrogative to a substantive
force is seen in English in such a sentence as, I know neither
the *how,* nor *why,* nor *when,* nor *where* of it. From its origin
in an adverbial interrogative of place, it comes to be that אַיִן is
primarily a negative of *existence* rather than of *action,* and is
therefore found most commonly and properly with nominal rather
than with verbal forms. The development of the negative
from *ay* has been carried much further than that from *m,* and
appears in several languages, while that from لـا is confined
with few exceptions to the Arabic. For a full presentation
of their development in Hebrew, see the Table E, Syntactical
Constructions.

The theory that makes the negatives אַיִן and لـا to be related
to the interrogative particles in the reverse order,* that is, that
the interrogatives were derived from the negative particles, which
has been shown to be etymologically improbable, can be shown
to be psychologically impossible. This has been done briefly by
Böttcher in his *Lehrbuch der hebräischen Sprache,* § 532 *sq.*
Taking the simple sentence אַיִן הוּא, and reading the אַיִן as the
rhetorical interrogative אַיֵּה־נָא, "where, pray, is he?" the impli-
cation is evident that *he is not,* as in the challenge of the Rab-
shakeh, 2 Kgs., 18:34, "Where are the gods of Hamath and
Arpad?" If now we read the אַיִן as originally negative, *he is not,*

* Gesenius-Rödiger, *Hebrew Grammar,* ed. by Conant, pp. 272 *sq.*

we may by the proper inflection indicate a question, *he is not?* =
is he not? but the question relates only to the existence of the
person; it asks nothing as to the *where?* The answer can only
be "yes" or "no." But the interrogative אַיֵּה, or, as in 2 Kgs.
20:14, מֵאַיִן יָבֹאוּ, " whence do they come?" and the Arabic أَيْنَ,
where? can never be answered by "yes" or "no." Being an
adverbial interrogative, it calls for an adverbial answer. "Where
is he?" asked with rhetorical inflection can easily and naturally
suggest, *he is not*; but "not is he?" can never by inflection or
by re-arrangement of the order of the words suggest the thought,
where is he?

The same reasoning applies to the substantive interrogative
مَا. The sentence, مَا ضَرَبَ زَيْد, "What did Zeid (ever) strike,"
with the proper rhetorical emphasis means, "Zeid has not (ever)
struck (anything);" but the same sentence rendered originally as
negative, "Zeid has not struck," can never by change of inflection or of order of words call for a substantive answer, which it
must do if rendered, "What has Zeid struck?" Examples might
be given to show that this holds equally good whether the مَا be
subject or predicate nominative, or object or adverbial accusative.

<h1 style="text-align:center">V.</h1>

THE SEMITIC CONCEPT OF NONENTITY.

Prof. Max Müller, in his *Lectures on the Science of Language*,
2d series, pp. 344–7, is at some pains to show that abstract
nothingness was inconceivable to the human mind until the
theologians invented it for use in their discussions on escha-
tology, and made annihilation their bugbear with which to
frighten men into being good. In demonstration of this he
arrays certain facts in Indo-European philology to show that the
nearest approach that language could make to expressing nonentity was by taking the smallest conceivable concrete thing or
actual existence, and then denying that object or existence.
Hence all words expressive of non-existence in the Indo-European
stock are necessarily compounds. Thus in English, *nothing* =
no thing and *none* = *no one;* in French, *ne . . . rien* = Latin *ne*
. . . rem, " not a thing " and *ne . . . . point* = Latin *ne . . . .*

punctum, "not a point;" in Italian, *niente* = Latin *ne* . . . . *ens*
for *essens*, "not being;" in Latin, *nihil*, from which *annihilation*,
= *ne filum*, "not a thread," by change of *f* to *h* frequently seen
in Spanish words borrowed from the Latin; in Greek, οὐδέν; and
in Sanskrit, *asat* = *a* privative and *sat* = Latin *sens* or *ens*,
"being."

The position seems well sustained by the Indo-European philology, but if Professor Müller had looked at the Hebrew, he
would have found that the Semitic mind, whether early or late,
whether in the clergy or the laity, grasped the idea of abstract
nonentity immediately and expressed it by its simplest uncompounded negative particles. Moreover, in Hebrew the terms are
not used eschatologically. It must be admitted that the simple
negative particles לֹא and אַל occur but rarely as substantives,
but this is because לֹא and אַל are primarily negatives of *action*,
not of *being*, whereas for the idea of nonentity a negative of
entity is wanted. This the Hebrew finds in its אַיִן, which,
though a compound indeed as an interrogative, is as a negative
to be considered a simple form, since the compounding took place
previous to its reaching the negative stage. The Hebrew, therefore, has expressions which for brevity and directness correspond,
not to our roundabout *nothingness*, *no-thing-ness*, but to our *notness*. The following are examples of the simple negative so used,
Isa. 55:2:

$$\text{לָמָּה תִשְׁקְלוּ כֶסֶף בְּלוֹא לֶחֶם}$$
$$\text{וִיגִיעֲכֶם בְּלוֹא לְשָׂבְעָה}$$

"Wherefore do ye spend money for the nothing (or notness) of
bread, and your labor for nothing for satisfying." Here if any
should prefer to take the לֹא לֶחֶם as a compound like לֹא דבר =
no-thing, or like the peculiar expressions, לֹא־עַמִּי and לֹא־רֻחָמָה
of Hos. 1:6, 9; we have yet the second phrase in which the לְ
before שָׂבְעָה cuts it off from compounding with לוֹא and leaves
the latter to stand by itself as a noun of nothingness in the absolute state. Dan. 4:32, וכל דָארֵי אַרְעָא כְּלָה חֲשִׁיבִין, "All the
inhabitants of the earth are reputed *as nothing*." Job 24:25,
מִי יַכְזִיבֵנִי וְיָשֵׂם לְאַל מִלָּתִי "Who will make me out a liar and put
my words *to naught?*"

Isa. 41:12, יהיו כאין "They shall be *as naught*."

Isa. 41:24, הן אתם מאין "Behold, ye are of *nothing*."

Amos 5:5, ובית אל יהיה לאון "And Bethel shall come to *nothingness*."

In addition to this use of the simple negative particle to express *nothingness*, the Hebrew employs in great variety verbal nouns such as תהו, אפס, אתה, הבל, ריק and בלתי to suggest the same idea, and also uses compounds in the same way as the Indo-European, as לא דבר and בלימה of Job 26:7 = *no-thing*, though in such cases more often the לא is separated from the noun by the verb or even by the entire remainder of the sentence, as in the very common constructions לא...כל, לא...איש and לא...דבר.

Table D.—*Occurrences of Negatives in the Old Testament.*

	לֹא (לא)	לֹא (אל)	אַל	בַּל	אֵין	אַיִן	עַד	בְּלִי	בֶּלִי	בִּלְתִּי	בְּלוֹ	אֶפֶס	מָאֵן	פֶּן	אוּלַי	אַיֵּה	אַיִן	אָפֵס	אַל	אַיִן אַיִן	לוּ
Gen. ...	212	..	39	1	36	..	..	1	8	3	10	2	..	17	..	4	..	1	..	3	10	10
Ex.	244	..	19	..	22	..	..	1	5	..	4	..	..	13	..	..	..	..	..	1	2	8
Lev. ...	282	..	11	..	21	..	..	..	3	..	1	..	..	1	..	..	..	..	..	..	3	..
Num. ..	188	..	14	..	19	..	..	..	7	1	1	2	..	3	..	1	..	..	..	..	..	2
Deut. ..	408	..	21	1	30	..	..	4	7	..	1	2	..	28	1	..	..	..	..	3	5	20
Josh....	98	..	20	..	5	..	..	1	9	1	2	..	..	3	1	..	..	..	..	..	9	15
Judg...	132	..	16	1	27	..	..	-2	4	..	1	1	..	5	..	..	..	2	..	2	..	7
1 Sam...	198	..	25	1	33	2	..	-6	2	..	5	..	..	7	1	5	..	2	..	2	8	2
2 Sam...	130	..	23	1	15	..	..	-4 (5)	3	2	..	2	..	6	1	6	..	..	..	..	6	..
1 Kgs...	177	..	13	..	25	..	..	-3	3	..	..	..	..	..	2	5	..	..	..	1	7	11
2 Kgs...	178	..	23	1	20	..	..	3	5	1	2	2	..	2	1	7	..	1	..	1	15	10
Isa.....	432	..	43	1	91	..	24	6	5	6	7	13	1	3	4	3	..	22	..	..	5	1
Jer.....	510	1	80	..	89	..	..	4	25	1	4	..	..	8	..	1	..	21	..	1	15	2
Ezek....	335	..	14	..	24	..	..	2	15	..	1	..	..	..	..	9	..	..	..	..	..	..
Hos. ...	67	..	7	..	15	2	..	4	1	..	..	..	..	1	1	..	..	..	..	..	..	..
Joel....	12	..	4	..	3	..	..	..	..	..	..	..	..	..	..	..	..	..	..	..	..	..
Amos...	72	..	2	..	5	..	..	..	2	..	..	2	..	1	..	1	..	..	..	1	2	1
Obad...	4	..	8	..	1	..	..	..	..	..	..	..	..	..	..	..	..	..	..	..	..	..
Jon.....	9	..	5	..	..	..	..	..	..	..	..	..	..	..	..	..	..	..	..	..	..	..
Mic	29	..	6	..	6	..	..	..	..	..	..	1	..	..	..	..	..	..	..	..	1	..
Nah....	9	..	..	..	7	..	..	-2	..	..	..	..	..	..	..	..	..	..	..	..	..	..
Hab. ...	21	..	..	..	3	..	..	..	..	..	..	..	..	..	..	..	..	..	..	..	..	..
Zeph. ..	25	..	2	..	3	..	..	2	..	..	3	1	..	..	..	..	..	4	..	..	..	..
Hag....	4	..	1	..	5	..	..	..	..	..	1	..	..	..	..	..	..	..	..	..	..	..
Zech. ..	51	..	7	..	4	..	..	..	..	..	..	..	..	1	..	..	..	4	..	..	1	..
Mal	19	..	1	..	6	..	..	1	..	..	..	..	..	1	..	..	..	1	..	..	..	..
Ps.......	329	..	122	6	66	..	30	-2 (6)	..	1	4	1	..	9	1	3	..	3	..	1	2	1
Prov....	134	..	89	..	37	..	10	-2	..	..	3	2	..	17	..	..	..	..	..	..	2	1
Job.....	290	..	24	..	29	1	..	18	1	1	1	1	..	1	..	3	..	7	..	..	..	..
Cant....	11	..	2	..	5	..	..	..	..	..	..	..	..	..	..	..	2	..	..	..	..	..
Ruth. ..	18	..	8	..	1	..	..	..	3	..	1	..	..	1	1	..	..	1	..	1	1	..
Lam. ..	30	..	5	..	11	..	..	1	..	..	..	..	..	..	..	2	..	..	..	..	..	..
Eccles..	65	..	21	..	44	..	..	1	..	..	..	..	..	..	..	..	..	..	..	1	3	..
Esth...	28	..	4	..	10	..	..	..	..	..	..	..	..	..	..	..	..	..	..	..	3	..
Dan. ...	45	69	6	..	9	..	..	..	2	..	..	1	..	..	..	..	..	2	..	..	..	..
Ezra ...	15	12	2	..	4	..	..	..	..	..	..	..	..	..	..	..	..	1	..	..	..	..
Neh	64	..	9	..	11	..	..	..	..	..	..	..	..	..	..	2	..	..	..	..	2	..
1 Chron.	53	..	7	..	9	..	1	..	1	..	..	..	..	1	1	..	..	..	..	1	3	..
2 Chron.	156	..	20	..	25	..	..	-1	1	..	..	..	..	..	..	..	..	..	..	3	4	6	11
Total...	5093	82	732	13	776	3	67	76	82	17	52	33	1	128	15	54	2					

NOTES ON TABLE OF OCCURRENCES.

לֹא. The enumeration includes all cases where other spellings, as לוֹ (1 Sam. 2:20) and לֹה (Deut. 3:11) are used for לֹא, all compounds of לֹא as הֲלֹא, בלא and ללא and both long and short forms. It includes also its occurrences in the asseverative אם לא, though its negative force is lost in the rendering "surely." It does not include לֹא = lā.

אַל includes also the two occurrences of אֵל (Isa. 37:10;* Jer. 51:3) and two of עַל for אַל (2 Kgs. 23:18; Ezek. 9:5).

אַיִן includes אֵין and אָיִן, but no case of אוֹן or אִי.

בַּל includes all cases where it has the meaning *not, lest* or *but* adversative, but not cases where it is merely affirmatively intensive = surely.

בְּלִי includes its use in the compound בְּלִיַּעַל, the number of such occurrences being indicated by a figure preceded by hyphen, to be understood as included in the larger figure when there are two. It includes also the one occurrence of בְּלִימָה (Job 26:7) and all compounds with prepositions.

בִּלְתִּי includes all forms of this in composition with the prepositions לְ, מִן, etc., and the case rendered "only" or in margin of R. V. "without me" (Isa. 10:4).

אפס includes the occurrences of the verb אָפֵס, to *not be*, the conjunction אפס כי *except that*, the use with pronominal suffixes as אפסי and as noun of *nothingness*, but does not include its use as a concrete noun as in אפסי ארץ *ends of the earth*, and אפסים *extremities, i. e.*, hands and feet.

אָפַע occurring but once (Isa. 41:24) is probably a corruption of אפס.

אִם includes only those occurrences where, though originally a conditional particle, it now has the force of a negative after formulæ of asseveration expressed or implied. It does not, however, include the אם of אם לא which, though of the same origin and force originally, becomes in connection with לא equivalent to the affirmative "surely." See note on לא.

מָה. The occurrence of מָה in rhetorical question is analogous to the use of ما in Arabic, but occurring far less frequently, can hardly be said to have become sufficiently common and stereotyped to have lost its original interrogative force. In two cases, however, Cant. 8:4, it replaces in similar construction the אם's of 2:7 and 3:5 which have the force of negative particles in adjuration. This seems the only case where we can fairly render מָה as a negative in the Hebrew.

רַק. כִּי אִם. כִּי. אֲבָל. מִן. The classification of these particles as negatives or adversatives being in many cases a matter of interpretation and opinion, the table enumerates only those cases that seem least

* Pointed with *pathah* in the Baer and Delitzsch text.

doubtful, and they are not summarized. Thus, מִן is originally partitive or comparative and after a verb implying separation must be rendered "from," as in the sentence "he prevented them *from speaking*." But in the sentence, Isa. 5:6, עַל הֶעָבִים אֲצַוֶּה מֵהַמְטִיר "I will command the clouds not to rain," the privative force is not so apparent in the principal verb, *will command*, and the particle may be rendered as negative. So also in the case of the other particles, the exact value in some cases is not determined and the enumeration cannot be definite.

Table E.—Syntactical Constructions of the Hebrew Negative.

לֹא

1. With finite verb, perf., Gen. 2:5, לֹא הִמְטִיר יְהֹוָה אֱלֹהִים

2. " " " imperf. declarative, Isa. 39:6, לֹא יִוָּתֵר דָּבָר

3. " " " " strong jussive, Gen. 2:17, לֹא תֹאכַל מִמֶּנּוּ

4. " " " " weak jussive, continuing אַל, Lev. 10:6,

רָאשֵׁיכֶם אַל תִּפְרָעוּ וּבִגְדֵיכֶם לֹא תִפְרֹמוּ

5. With finite verb, in asseveration = אִם,

Ezek. 14:18, חַי־אָנִי נְאֻם אֲדֹנָי יְהֹוִה אִם יַצִּילוּ בָּנִים

6. With noun, Jer. 18:17, עֹרֶף וְלֹא־פָנִים אֶרְאֵם

7. " " in nominal sentence, Gen. 42:34, כִּי לֹא מְרַגְּלִים אַתֶּם

8. " " negating a quality, 2 Chron. 13:9, "that which is a no-god," = noun in construct, וְהָיָה כֹהֵן לְלֹא אֱלֹהִים

9. With adjective, Ex. 22:15, בְּתוּלָה אֲשֶׁר לֹא אֹרָשָׂה

10. " " phrase, Gen. 15:13, בְּאֶרֶץ לֹא לָהֶם

11. With adverb, Gen. 48:18, וַיֹּאמֶר יוֹסֵף . . . לֹא־כֵן אָבִי

12. " " phrase, Ex. 3:19, וְלֹא בְּיָד חֲזָקָה

13. With noun as jussive = אַל, Prov. 27:2,

יְהַלֶּלְךָ זָר וְלֹא פִיךָ נָכְרִי וְאַל שְׂפָתֶיךָ

14. Independent = *nay!* Gen. 19:2 (kethibh), וַיֹּאמְרוּ לֹא כִּי בָרְחוֹב נָלִין

15. With sentence, Ezek. 18:29, הֲלֹא דַרְכֵיכֶם לֹא יִתָּכֵן

16. After preposition בְּ with (a) noun = *without*, Jer. 22:13,

הוֹי בֹּנֶה בֵיתוֹ בְלֹא־צֶדֶק

" " " " (b) verb imperf., Lam. 4:14,

בְּלֹא יוּכְלוּ יִגְּעוּ בִּלְבֻשֵׁיהֶם

" " " " (c) verb. infin., Num. 35:23,

בְּכֹל אֶבֶן אֲשֶׁר יָמוּת בָּהּ בְּלֹא רְאוֹת

After preposition בְּ with (d) prep. and noun, Isa. 55:2, בְּלוֹא לְשָׂבְעָה

"   "   "   " (e) adv. phrase, 2 Chron. 30:18,

אָכְלוּ אֶת־הַפֶּסַח בְּלֹא כַכָּתוּב

17. After preposition לְ with (a) finite perf., Isa. 65:1,

נִמְצֵאתִי לְלֹא בִקְשֻׁנִי

"   "   "   " (b) adj. phrase, Job 39:16,

הִקְשִׁיחַ בָּנֶיהָ לְּלֹא־לָהּ

18. After preposition עַל with finite perf., Ps. 119:136,

פַּלְגֵי מַיִם יָרְדוּ עֵינָי עַל לֹא־שָׁמְרוּ תוֹרָתֶךָ

19. After preposition כְּ with finite perf., Obad. 16, וְהָיוּ כְּלוֹא הָיוּ

20. After preposition פֶּן = לְבִּי , Ps. 119:80, לְבִּי לֹא אֵבוֹשׁ

21. Followed by לְ with infin. = οὐκ ἔστι, Amos 6:10,

הָס כִּי לֹא לְהַזְכִּיר בְּשֵׁם יְהוָֹה

22. With יֵשׁ = Arab. لَيْسَ , Job 9:33, לֹא יֵשׁ בֵּינֵינוּ מוֹכִיחַ

23. "   אִם = assuredly, Gen. 24:38, אִם־לֹא אֶל־בֵּית־אָבִי תֵלֵךְ

24. "   הֲ־ independent = Germ. nicht wahr? Judg. 14:15,

הַלְיָרְשֵׁנוּ קְרָאתֶם לָנוּ הֲלֹא

אַל

1. Deprecation, finite imperf., Gen. 13:8,

אַל־נָא תְהִי מְרִיבָה בֵּינִי וּבֵינֶךָ

2. "   nominal sentence, 2 Sam. 1:21,

הָרֵי בַגִּלְבֹּעַ אַל־טַל וְאַל מָטָר עֲלֵיכֶם

3. Nominal sentence declarative, Prov. 12:28,

בְּאֹרַח צְדָקָה חַיִּים וְדֶרֶךְ נְתִיבָה אַל־מָוֶת

4. As substantive, Job 24:25, מִי יַכְזִיבֵנִי וְיָשֵׂם לְאַל מִלָּתִי

5. Independent = nay! Gen. 19:18, וַיֹּאמֶר לוֹט אֲלֵהֶם אַל־נָא אֲדֹנָי

אַיִן.

1. Construct state with noun, Gen. 37:29, אֵין יוֹסֵף בַּבּוֹר

2. "   "   " pronoun, Gen. 28:17, אֵין זֶה כִּי אִם בֵּית אֱלֹהִים

3. "   "   " suffix, Gen. 37:30, הַיֶּלֶד אֵינֶנּוּ

4. "   "   " before participle = copula, Gen. 20:7,

וְאִם אֵינְךָ מֵשִׁיב

5. "   "   " adj. phrase, Ex. 8:6, אֵין כַּיהוָֹה אֱלֹהֵינוּ

6. Construct state with noun and governed by בִּן, Isa. 6:11, מֵאֵין אָדָם

7.   "   "   "   inf. and governed by בִּן, Mal. 2:13,

מֵאֵין עוֹד פְּנוֹת

8.   "   "   "   adj. phrase and governed by בִּן, Jer. 10:6,

מֵאֵין כָּמוֹךָ

9.   "   "   "   noun and governed by בְּ, Ezek. 38:11,

בְּאֵין חוֹמָה

10.   "   "   "   "   "   "   " לְ, Isa. 40:29,

וּלְאֵין אוֹנִים עָצְמָה יַרְבֶּה

11.   "   "   "   participle and governed by לְ, Neh. 8:10,

וְשִׁלְחוּ מָנוֹת לְאֵין נָכוֹן לוֹ

12.   "   "   "   noun and strengthened by עוֹד, Isa. 23:10,

אֵין מֵזַח עוֹד

13.   "   "   "   noun separated by עוֹד, Jer. 49:7,

הַאֵין עוֹד חָכְמָה בְּתֵימָן

14.   "   "   "   infin. with לְ = οὐκ ἔστι, Eccles. 3:14,

עָלָיו אֵין לְהוֹסִיף וּמִמֶּנּוּ אֵין לִגְרֹעַ

15.   "   "   "   adv. phrase or obj. acc.(?), Hag. 2:17,

וְאֵין אֶתְכֶם אֵלַי

16.   "   "   "   יֵשׁ pleonastic, Ps. 135:17, אֵין יֵשׁ רוּחַ בְּפִיהֶם

17.   "   "   "   noun and after בְּלִי pleonastic, 2 Kgs. 1:3,

הֲמִבְּלִי אֵין אֱלֹהִים בְּיִשְׂרָאֵל

18.   "   "   between partic. noun and its object, Gen. 40:8,

חֲלוֹם חָלַמְנוּ וּפֹתֵר אֵין אֹתוֹ

19.   "   "   "   noun and adv. phrase = copula, Gen. 19:31,

וְאִישׁ אֵין בָּאָרֶץ

20. Absolute state between noun and adv. phrase, 2 Kgs. 19:3,

וְכֹחַ אַיִן לְלֵדָה

21.   "   "   after noun, Lev. 26:37, וְרֹדֵף אָיִן

22.   "   "   independent, 1 Kgs. 18:10, וְאָמְרוּ אָיִן

23.   "   "   after preposition = substantive;—with לְ, Isa. 40:23,

הַנּוֹתֵן רוֹזְנִים לְאָיִן

24.   "   "   "   "   = substantive;—with כְּ, Hag. 2:3,

הֲלוֹא כָמֹהוּ כְּאַיִן בְּעֵינֵיכֶם

25.   "   "   "   "   = adv. phrase = *almost*, Ps. 73:2,

רַגְלָי כְּאַיִן שֻׁפְּכָה

26. Absolute state after preposition = subst.; — with מִן, Isa. 41:24,

הֵן־אַתֶּם מֵאַיִן וּפָעָלְכֶם מֵאָפַע

27.   "   "   "   "   and followed by adj. phrase, Jer. 30:7

(but cf. Jer. 10:6, note 8 above), גָּדוֹל הַיּוֹם הַהוּא מֵאַיִן כָּמֹהוּ

28. Absolute state with verb perfect = לֹא, Job 35:15,

וְעַתָּה כִּי אַיִן פָּקַד אַפּוֹ וְלֹא־יָדַע בַּפַּשׁ

אִי

1. With noun, 1 Sam. 4:21, אִי כָבוֹד
2.   "   adjective, Job 22:30, אִי־נָקִי

בְּלִי

1. With noun = without, Isa. 28:8, בְּלִי מָקוֹם
2.   "   adjective, 2 Sam. 1:21, מָגֵן שָׁאוּל בְּלִי מָשִׁיחַ בַּשָּׁמֶן
3.   "   finite verb perfect, Gen. 31:20, עַל בְּלִי הִגִּיד לוֹ כִּי בֹרֵחַ הוּא
4.   "   "   "   imperf., Hos. 8:7, בְּלִי יַעֲשֶׂה־קֶּמַח
5. In composition with noun, Judg. 19:22, בְּלִיַּעַל
6.   "   "   "   pronoun, Job 26:7, עַל בְּלִי־מָה
7.   "   "   "   preposition, with בְּ, Deut. 4:42,

יִרְצַח אֶת־רֵעֵהוּ בִּבְלִי־דַעַת

8.   "   "   "   "   " לְ, Isa. 5:14,

וּפָעֲרָה פִיהָ לִבְלִי־חֹק

9.   "   "   "   "   " מִן with noun, Jer. 2:15,

מִבְּלִי יֹשֵׁב

10.   "   "   "   "   "   " infin., Deut. 9:28,

מִבְּלִי יְכֹלֶת יְהֹוָה לַהֲבִיאָם אֶל הָאָרֶץ

11.   "   "   " מִן with adj. phrase, Job 18:15,

תִּשְׁכּוֹן בְּאָהֳלוֹ מִבְּלִי לוֹ

12.   "   "   " מִן and with אֵין pleonastic, Ex. 14:11,

הֲמִבְּלִי אֵין־קְבָרִים בְּמִצְרַיִם

13. As substantive = nothingness, "the pit," Isa. 38:17,

וְאַתָּה חָשַׁקְתָּ נַפְשִׁי מִשַּׁחַת בְּלִי

בִּלְתִּי

1. With noun = except, Gen. 21:26, לֹא שָׁמַעְתִּי בִּלְתִּי הַיּוֹם
2.   "   adj. phrase = only, Num. 11:6, בִּלְתִּי אֶל־הַמָּן עֵינֵינוּ

3. With pronom. suffix, 1 Sam. 2:2, כִּי אֵין בִּלְתֶּךָ
4. "   "   "   hidden, Hos. 13:4, "And deliverer there is none except me," וּמוֹשִׁיעַ אַיִן בִּלְתִּי
5. "   אִם = *except*, Gen. 47:18, לֹא נִשְׁאַר לִפְנֵי אֲדֹנִי בִּלְתִּי אִם־גְּוִיָּתֵנוּ
6. "   nominal sentence, Gen. 43:5, לֹא־תִרְאוּ פָנַי בִּלְתִּי אֲחִיכֶם אִתְּכֶם
7. Independent = *nay!* Dan. 11:18(?), בִּלְתִּי חֶרְפָּתוֹ יָשִׁיב לוֹ
8. With preposition עַד before finite verb perf., Num. 21:35,

וַיַּכּוּ אֹתוֹ ... עַד־בִּלְתִּי הִשְׁאִיר לוֹ שָׂרִיד

9. "   "   לְ before infin., Gen. 4:15,

לְבִלְתִּי הַכּוֹת אֹתוֹ כָּל־מֹצְאוֹ

10. "   "   "   "   finite perf., Jer. 23:14,

לְבִלְתִּי שָׁבוּ אִישׁ מֵרָעָתוֹ

11. "   "   "   "   "   imperf., Ex. 20:20, לְבִלְתִּי תֶחֱטָאוּ
12. "   "   "   "   לְ and infin., 2 Kgs. 23:10,

לְבִלְתִּי לְהַעֲבִיר אִישׁ אֶת־בְּנוֹ ... בָּאֵשׁ

13. "   "   מִן "   infin., Num. 14:16 (*cf.* under בְּלִי, No. 10, Deut. 9:28), מִבִּלְתִּי יְכֹלֶת יְהֹוָה לְהָבִיא אֶת־הָעָם

בַּל

1. With adjective, Prov. 24:23, בְּמִשְׁפָּט בַּל־טוֹב
2. "   "   phrase, Prov. 23:7, לִבּוֹ בַּל־עִמָּךְ
3. "   finite perfect, Isa. 26:10, יֻחַן רָשָׁע בַּל לָמַד צֶדֶק
4. "   "   imperf., Isa. 26:10, וּבַל יִרְאֶה גֵּאוּת
5. "   infinitive = פֶּן, Ps. 32:9, בַּל קְרֹב אֵלֶיךָ

בִּלְעֲדֵי

1. = *except*, Gen. 14:24, בִּלְעָדַי רַק אֲשֶׁר אָכְלוּ הַנְּעָרִים
2. = *not by me*, Gen. 41:16, בִּלְעָדָי אֱלֹהִים יַעֲנֶה אֶת־שְׁלוֹם פַּרְעֹה
3. With preposition מִן = *besides*, Josh. 22:19,

בִּבְנֹתְכֶם לָכֶם מִזְבֵּחַ מִבַּלְעֲדֵי מִזְבַּח יְהֹוָה אֱלֹהֵינוּ

טֶרֶם

1. With finite perf., Gen. 24:15, וַיְהִי־הוּא טֶרֶם כִּלָּה לְדַבֵּר
2. "   "   imperf., Ex. 9:30, יָדַעְתִּי כִּי טֶרֶם תִּירְאוּן מִפְּנֵי יְהֹוָה

3. With finite imperf. for בְּטֶרֶם , Ex. 12:34,

וַיִּשָּׂא הָעָם אֶת־בְּצֵקוֹ טֶרֶם יֶחְמָץ

4.   "   preposition בְּ and followed by perfect, Ps. 90:2,

בְּטֶרֶם הָרִים יֻלָּדוּ

5.   "   "   "   "   "   " imperf., Gen. 27:4,

תְּבָרֶכְךָ נַפְשִׁי בְּטֶרֶם אָמוּת

6.   "   "   " before noun, Isa. 17:14, בְּטֶרֶם בֹּקֶר אֵינֶנּוּ

7.   "   "   "   " infin., Zeph. 2:2,

בְּטֶרֶם לֶדֶת חֹק כְּמוֹץ עָבַר יוֹם

8.   "   "   מִן before infin., Hag. 2:15,

מִטֶּרֶם שׂוּם־אֶבֶן אֶל־אָבֶן

9.   "   "   בְּ and לֹא pleonastic, Zeph. 2:2,

בְּטֶרֶם לֹא יָבוֹא עֲלֵיכֶם חֲרוֹן

אֶפֶס

1. With noun = *only*, Num. 22:35,

וְאֶפֶס אֶת־הַדָּבָר אֲשֶׁר־אֲדַבֵּר אֵלֶיךָ אֹתוֹ תְדַבֵּר

2.   " adjective = substantive, 2 Kgs. 14:26, אֶפֶס עָצוּר וְאֶפֶס עָזוּב

3.   " adverbial phrase, Isa. 54:15, גּוּר יָגוּר אֶפֶס מֵאוֹתִי

4.   " pronominal suffix, Isa. 47:10, אֲנִי וְאַפְסִי עוֹד

5.   " כִּי as conjunction = *but, except that*, Deut. 15:4,

אֶפֶס כִּי לֹא יִהְיֶה

6.   " preposition מִן = substantive, Isa. 40:17, מֵאֶפֶס וָתֹהוּ

7.   "   " בְּ = substantive, Prov. 14:28,

וּבְאֶפֶס לְאֹם מְחִתַּת רָזוֹן

8. As verb, Gen. 47:15, כִּי אָפֵס כָּסֶף

פֶּן

1. With perfect, clause of possibility, 2 Kgs. 2:16,

וִיבַקְשׁוּ אֶת־אֲדֹנֶיךָ פֶּן נְשָׂאוֹ רוּחַ יְהֹוָה

2.   " imperf., of caution, Gen. 3:22, פֶּן יִשְׁלַח יָדוֹ

3.   "   " of adjuration = אִם, Judg. 15:12,

הִשָּׁבְעוּ לִי פֶּן תִּפְגְּעוּן בִּי אַתֶּם

4.   "   " of mild prohibition = אַל, Jer. 51:46, וּפֶן יֵרַךְ לְבַבְכֶם

5.   " omission of verb, Prov. 25:8,

אַל תֵּצֵא לָרִב מַהֵר פֶּן מַה־תַּעֲשֶׂה בְּאַחֲרִיתָהּ

זוּלַת

1. With noun = *only*, Deut. 4:12,   וּתְמוּנָה אֵינְכֶם רֹאִים זוּלָתִי קוֹל

2.   "   pronominal suffix = *except*, 1 Sam. 21:10,

כִּי אֵין אַחֶרֶת זוּלָתָהּ בָּזֶה

אִם

1. In asseveration with imperfect, Gen. 42:15,   חֵי פַרְעֹה אִם־תֵּצְאוּ מִזֶּה

2.   "   "   " nouns, Ezek. 14:16,

חַי אָנִי נְאֻם אֲדֹנָי יְהוִֹה אִם־בָּנִים וְאִם־בָּנוֹת יַצִּילוּ

3.   "   "   after חָלִילָה , imperf., Job 27:5,

חָלִילָה לִּי אִם אַצְדִּיק אֶתְכֶם

4.   " adjuration, imperf., Cant. 2:7,

הִשְׁבַּעְתִּי אֶתְכֶם . . . אִם תָּעִירוּ . . . אֶת־הָאַהֲבָה

מַה

In adjuration, imperf., Cant. 8:4 (*cf.* under אִם , No. 4 above),

הִשְׁבַּעְתִּי אֶתְכֶם . . . מַה־תָּעִירוּ . . . אֶת־הָאַהֲבָה

VITA.

I, Dean A. Walker, was born at Diarbekr, Turkey, on February 3, 1860. I studied in the public schools of Newton, Mass., from 1867–1880, at Yale University from 1880–84. After this, I was for the period of one year, Instructor in the Hopkins Grammar School at New Haven; Professor of Languages in Colorado College, 1885–86; and entered the Yale Divinity School in 1886, where I remained until 1889. From 1889–92 I was Asssistant and Principal of the Preparatory Department of the Syrian Protestant College at Beirut, Syria. Shortly after my return to America in 1893, I entered The University of Chicago as a Graduate Student in the Semitic Department and acted as a University Extension Lecturer. During the Summer of 1894 and 1895 I was Lecturer for the American Institute of Sacred Literature at the Chautauqua Assemblies. Since Autumn of 1895, I am Professor of English Bible and Instructor in Social Science at Wells College, Aurora, N. Y. To my former teachers at Yale University and in The University of Chicago, who have always assisted me with kind advice and assistance, I herewith express my grateful thanks.

www.ingramcontent.com/pod-product-compliance
Lightning Source LLC
Chambersburg PA
CBHW021445090426
42739CB00009B/1649